C000235949

YOU'RE NOT OLD

YOU'RE
Vintage

summersdale

YOU'RE NOT OLD, YOU'RE VINTAGE

This edition copyright © Octopus Publishing Group Limited, 2024
First edition published in 2014
Second edition published in 2017

An Hachette UK Company
www.hachette.co.uk

Summersdale Publishers
Part of Octopus Publishing Group Limited
Carmelite House
50 Victoria Embankment
LONDON
EC4Y 0DZ
UK

www.summersdale.com

Printed and bound in China

ISBN: 978-1-83799-356-7

Substantial discounts on bulk quantities of Summersdale books are available to corporations, professional associations and other organizations. For details contact general enquiries: telephone: +44 (0) 1243 771107 or email: enquiries@summersdale.com.

TO ....

FROM ....

You don't get older,
you get better.

SHIRLEY BASSEY

WITH MIRTH AND LAUGHTER LET OLD WRINKLES COME.

WILLIAM SHAKESPEARE

Eventually you will reach a point when you stop lying about your age and start bragging about it.

WILL ROGERS

YOU CAN'T TURN BACK THE CLOCK. BUT YOU CAN WIND IT UP AGAIN.

BONNIE PRUDDEN

Laughter is timeless,
imagination has no
age, and dreams
are forever.

WALT DISNEY

GROW OLD ALONG
WITH ME! THE BEST
IS YET TO BE.

ROBERT BROWNING

The good old
days are now.

TOM CLANCY

THE THREE AGES
OF MAN: YOUTH,
MIDDLE AGE, AND
"MY WORD YOU
DO LOOK WELL."

JUNE WHITFIELD

Nice to be here?
At my age it's nice
to be anywhere.

GEORGE BURNS

THERE'S NO SUCH THING AS AGEING, BUT MATURING AND KNOWLEDGE. IT'S BEAUTIFUL, I CALL THAT BEAUTY.

CELINE DION

What a wonderful life
I've had! I only wish
I'd realized it sooner.

COLETTE

AGE IS AN ISSUE OF
MIND OVER MATTER.
IF YOU DON'T MIND,
IT DOESN'T MATTER.

ANONYMOUS

If wrinkles must be
written upon our
brows, let them not
be written upon
the heart. The spirit
should never grow old.

JAMES A. GARFIELD

THE BEST TIME TO
PLANT A TREE WAS
TWENTY YEARS
AGO. THE SECOND
BEST TIME IS NOW.

CHINESE PROVERB

I've never felt
so powerful and so
calm. I just don't
care, because I'm
too old. It's such
a great feeling.

EMMA THOMPSON

THE OLD AGE
OF AN EAGLE
IS BETTER THAN
THE YOUTH OF
A SPARROW.

GREEK PROVERB

I want to live to be one hundred and twenty. That's when I will start worrying about my age.

HELENA CHRISTENSEN

THE BEST TUNES
ARE PLAYED ON THE
OLDEST FIDDLES.

RALPH WALDO EMERSON

Whenever the talk
turns to age, I say
I am forty-nine
plus VAT.

LIONEL BLAIR

WHAT I HAVE LEARNED
SO FAR ABOUT
AGEING, DESPITE
THE CREAKINESS OF
ONE'S BONES AND
CRAGGINESS OF ONE'S
ONCE-SILKEN SKIN,
IS THIS: DO IT. BY
ALL MEANS, DO IT.

MAYA ANGELOU

Getting older
makes you
more alive.

JAMIE LEE CURTIS

GROWING OLD IS COMPULSORY; GROWING UP IS OPTIONAL.

BOB MONKHOUSE

It's important
to have a twinkle
in your wrinkle.

ANONYMOUS

WITH AGE COMES A LOT OF WISDOM, AND I'M HAPPIER NOW THAN I'VE EVER BEEN.

JADA PINKETT SMITH

We are always the
same age inside.

GERTRUDE STEIN

THE SECRET TO
STAYING YOUNG IS
TO LIVE HONESTLY,
EAT SLOWLY AND LIE
ABOUT YOUR AGE.

LUCILLE BALL

One of the good
things about getting
older is you find you're
more interesting
than most of the
people you meet.

LEE MARVIN

I LOVE EVERYTHING
THAT IS OLD: OLD
FRIENDS, OLD TIMES,
OLD MANNERS,
OLD BOOKS,
OLD WINE.

OLIVER GOLDSMITH

Youth has
no age.

PABLO PICASSO

TO ME, OLD AGE IS ALWAYS FIFTEEN YEARS OLDER THAN I AM.

BERNARD BARUCH

Old age is like
everything else.
To make a success
of it, you've got
to start young.

THEODORE ROOSEVELT

PEOPLE ARE AFRAID OF CHANGING; THAT THEY'RE LOSING SOMETHING. THEY DON'T UNDERSTAND THAT THEY ARE ALSO GAINING SOMETHING.

SHARON STONE

I don't feel old. I don't feel anything till noon. That's when it's time for my nap.

BOB HOPE

I LIKE THE WAY I LOOK. I LIKE THE WAY I FEEL. I LIKE MY ENERGY. I HAVE WISDOM. I HAVE PERSPECTIVE, AND I CAN TELL YOU THAT AGEING CAN BE SO INCREDIBLE.

SUZANNE SOMERS

The man of
wisdom is the
man of years.

EDWARD YOUNG

YOUTH DISSERVES;
MIDDLE AGE
CONSERVES; OLD
AGE PRESERVES.

MARTIN H. FISCHER

Growing older gracefully means having a keen curiosity about learning things about the world that you didn't know yesterday, no matter how many yesterdays you've had.

PADMA LAKSHMI

I'LL KEEP SWIVELLING
MY HIPS UNTIL THEY
NEED REPLACING.

TOM JONES

Your wrinkles reflect
the roads you have taken;
they form the map of your
life [...] My face carries
all my memories. Why
should I erase them?

DIANE VON **FURSTENBERG**

EVERYBODY SPOILS
YOU LIKE MAD AND
THEY TREAT YOU
WITH SUCH RESPECT
BECAUSE YOU'RE
OLD. LITTLE DO
THEY KNOW, YOU
HAVEN'T CHANGED.

BETTY WHITE

One of the best parts of growing older? You can flirt all you like since you've become harmless.

LIZ SMITH

AGE HOLDS ABSOLUTELY NO FEAR FOR ME. THERE IS SO MUCH ENJOYMENT AHEAD.

PENELOPE CRUZ

Just remember,
when you're over
the hill, you begin
to pick up speed.

CHARLES M. SCHULZ

OLD MEN ARE FOND
OF GIVING GOOD
ADVICE, TO CONSOLE
THEMSELVES FOR
BEING NO LONGER IN
A POSITION TO GIVE
BAD EXAMPLES.

FRANÇOIS DE LA
ROCHEFOUCAULD

I'm not sure
that old age
isn't the best
part of life.

C. S. LEWIS

THE WHITER
MY HAIR BECOMES,
THE MORE READY
PEOPLE ARE
TO BELIEVE
WHAT I SAY.

BERTRAND RUSSELL

As we grow older,
our bodies get
shorter and our
anecdotes longer.

ROBERT QUILLEN

WHEN YOU'RE YOUNG
AND BEAUTIFUL,
YOU'RE PARANOID
AND MISERABLE. I
THINK ONE OF THE
GREAT ADVANTAGES
OF GETTING OLDER
IS THAT YOU LET GO
OF CERTAIN THINGS.

HELEN MIRREN

When grace is joined
with wrinkles, it is
adorable. There is an
unspeakable dawn
in happy old age.

VICTOR HUGO

I ABSOLUTELY REFUSE
TO REVEAL MY AGE.
WHAT AM I — A CAR?

CYNDI LAUPER

A prune is a plum
with experience.

JOHN H. TRATTNER

SOME PEOPLE REACH THE AGE OF SIXTY BEFORE OTHERS.

SAMUEL HOOD

You can only
be young once.
But you can always
be immature.

DAVE BARRY

EVERY YEAR SHOULD
TEACH YOU SOMETHING
VALUABLE; WHETHER
YOU GET THE LESSON IS
UP TO YOU. EVERY YEAR
BRINGS YOU CLOSER TO
EXPRESSING YOUR WHOLE
AND HEALED SELF.

OPRAH WINFREY

There's one
advantage to being
one hundred and
two. There's no
peer pressure.

DENNIS WOLFBERG

THE COMBINATION
OF MY LEARNING,
MATURING AND
EARNING MY
WRINKLES, COMBINED
WITH THE WAY I
LOOK, I BELIEVE IS
THE BEST BALANCE
I HAVE EVER HAD.

PAULINA PORIZKOVA

Time and trouble will tame an advanced young woman, but an advanced old woman is uncontrollable by any earthly force.

DOROTHY L. SAYERS

THE AGEING
PROCESS HAS YOU
FIRMLY IN ITS GRASP
IF YOU NEVER GET
THE URGE TO THROW
A SNOWBALL.

DOUG LARSON

It is sad to grow old,
but nice to ripen.

BRIGITTE BARDOT

I'M AIMING BY
THE TIME I'M FIFTY
TO STOP BEING AN
ADOLESCENT.

WENDY COPE

It's wonderful to know you're ageing, because that means you're still on the planet, right?

GOLDIE HAWN

**AGE ISN'T
HOW OLD YOU ARE
BUT HOW OLD
YOU FEEL.**

GABRIEL GARCÍA
MÁRQUEZ

A birthday is just the first day of another 365-day journey around the sun. Enjoy the trip.

ANONYMOUS

WE DON'T STOP
PLAYING BECAUSE
WE GROW OLD;
WE GROW OLD
BECAUSE WE
STOP PLAYING.

GEORGE BERNARD SHAW

If I had my life to live
over again, I'd make
the same mistakes,
only sooner.

TALLULAH BANKHEAD

I WILL NEVER
GIVE IN TO OLD AGE
UNTIL I BECOME OLD.
AND I'M NOT OLD YET!

TINA TURNER

Cherish all your
happy moments;
they make a fine
cushion for old age.

CHRISTOPHER MORLEY

YOUTH IS THE TIME
FOR ADVENTURES OF
THE BODY, BUT AGE
FOR THE TRIUMPHS
OF THE MIND.

LOGAN PEARSALL SMITH

Allow me to put
the record straight.
I am forty-six and
have been for
some years past.

ERICA JONG

EVERYONE IS THE AGE OF THEIR HEART.

GUATEMALAN PROVERB

I feel the older I get,
the more I'm learning
to handle life. Being
on this quest for a
long time, it's all about
finding yourself.

RINGO STARR

I INTEND TO
LIVE FOREVER,
OR DIE TRYING.

GROUCHO MARX

Each year
it grows harder to
make ends meet –
the ends I refer to
are hands and feet.

RICHARD ARMOUR

MY GRANDMOTHER
IS OVER EIGHTY
AND STILL DOESN'T
NEED GLASSES.
DRINKS RIGHT OUT
OF THE BOTTLE.

HENNY YOUNGMAN

Another belief of
mine: that everyone
else my age is an
adult, whereas I am
merely in disguise.

MARGARET ATWOOD

I'M HAPPY TO REPORT THAT MY INNER CHILD IS STILL AGELESS.

JAMES BROUGHTON

Age is no barrier.
It's a limitation you
put on your mind.

JACKIE JOYNER-KERSEE

WHITE HAIR OFTEN
COVERS THE HEAD,
BUT THE HEART
THAT HOLDS IT IS
EVER YOUNG.

HONORÉ DE BALZAC

I don't believe in ageing. I believe in forever altering one's aspect to the sun.

VIRGINIA WOOLF

AGE SELDOM
ARRIVES SMOOTHLY
OR QUICKLY. IT'S
MORE OFTEN
A SUCCESSION
OF JERKS.

JEAN RHYS

Confidence comes
with age, and
looking beautiful
comes from the
confidence someone
has in themselves.

KATE WINSLET

AGE IS JUST
A NUMBER. IT'S
TOTALLY IRRELEVANT
UNLESS, OF COURSE,
YOU HAPPEN TO BE
A BOTTLE OF WINE.

JOAN COLLINS

I hope you are
as fun-loving and
adventurous as me
when you're my age!

MADONNA

THE OLDER YOU GET, THE BETTER YOU USED TO BE.

JOHN McENROE

My husband's idea
of a good night out
is a good night in.

MAUREEN LIPMAN

TO GET BACK MY
YOUTH I'D DO
ANYTHING IN THE
WORLD, EXCEPT
GET UP EARLY, TAKE
EXERCISE OR BE
RESPECTABLE.

OSCAR WILDE

I believe in loyalty.
When a woman
reaches a certain
age she likes, she
should stick with it.

EVA GABOR

OLD AGE AND
TREACHERY WILL
ALWAYS BEAT YOUTH
AND EXUBERANCE.

DAVID MAMET

The key to
successful ageing
is to pay as little
attention to it
as possible.

JUDITH REGAN

I PLAN ON GROWING
OLD MUCH LATER
IN LIFE, OR MAYBE
NOT AT ALL.

PATTY CAREY

I'm too old to do
things by half.

LOU REED

FUN IS LIKE LIFE INSURANCE; THE OLDER YOU GET, THE MORE IT COSTS.

KIN HUBBARD

I don't think about my life in terms of numbers. First of all, I ain't never gonna be old because I ain't got time to be old. I can't stop long enough to grow old.

DOLLY PARTON

IN YOUTH WE RUN INTO DIFFICULTIES. IN OLD AGE DIFFICULTIES RUN INTO US.

BEVERLY SILLS

To stop ageing –
keep on raging.

MICHAEL FORBES

WE TURN NOT OLDER WITH YEARS, BUT NEWER EVERY DAY.

EMILY DICKINSON

All would live
long, but none
would be old.

BENJAMIN FRANKLIN

AGE IS ONLY A NUMBER.

LEXI STARLING

Anyone who
keeps the ability
to see beauty
never grows old.

FRANZ KAFKA

I DON'T THINK
OF GETTING OLDER
AS LOOKING BETTER
OR WORSE; IT'S
JUST DIFFERENT.
YOU CHANGE, AND
THAT'S OKAY. LIFE
IS ABOUT CHANGE.

HEIDI KLUM

I must be
getting old.
I can't take yes
for an answer.

FRED ALLEN

WHEN IT COMES
TO STAYING YOUNG,
A MINDLIFT BEATS
A FACELIFT ANY DAY.

MARTY BUCELLA

Here is my biggest
takeaway after sixty
years on the planet:
there is great value
in being fearless.

DIANE KEATON

GROWING OLD IS NO MORE THAN A BAD HABIT WHICH A BUSY MAN HAS NO TIME TO FORM.

ANDRÉ MAUROIS

Oh, the worst of all tragedies is not to die young, but to live until I am seventy-five and yet not ever truly to have lived.

MARTIN LUTHER KING JR.

AUTUMN IS THE MELLOWER SEASON, AND WHAT WE LOSE IN FLOWERS, WE MORE THAN GAIN IN FRUITS.

SAMUEL BUTLER

You are never too
old to set another
goal or to dream
a new dream.

LES BROWN

OLD AGE ISN'T SO BAD
WHEN YOU CONSIDER
THE ALTERNATIVE.

MAURICE CHEVALIER

If you rest,
you rust.

HELEN HAYES

YOU CAN JUDGE
YOUR AGE BY THE
AMOUNT OF PAIN
YOU FEEL WHEN YOU
COME IN CONTACT
WITH A NEW IDEA.

PEARL S. BUCK

I can honestly say
I love getting older.
Then again, I never
put my glasses on
before looking in
the mirror.

CHERIE LUNGHI

MEN ARE LIKE
WINE – SOME TURN
TO VINEGAR, BUT
THE BEST IMPROVE
WITH AGE.

C. E. M. JOAD

Growing old is
not growing up.

DOUGLAS HORTON

LIVE YOUR LIFE AND FORGET YOUR AGE.

NORMAN VINCENT PEALE

Old age is like a plane flying through a storm. Once you are aboard there is nothing you can do.

GOLDA MEIR

COUNT YOUR AGE BY
FRIENDS, NOT YEARS.
COUNT YOUR LIFE BY
SMILES, NOT TEARS.

DIXIE WILLSON

The older I get,
the older old is.

TOM BAKER

ALAS, AFTER A
CERTAIN AGE EVERY
MAN IS RESPONSIBLE
FOR HIS FACE.

ALBERT CAMUS

I don't plan to grow old gracefully. I plan to have facelifts until my ears meet.

RITA RUDNER

YOU KNOW
YOU'RE GETTING
OLD WHEN THE
CANDLES COST MORE
THAN THE CAKE.

BOB HOPE

Older people
shouldn't eat health
food, they need all
the preservatives
they can get.

ROBERT ORBEN

I'M SIXTY
YEARS OF AGE.
THAT'S 16 CELSIUS!

GEORGE CARLIN

You can't help
getting older,
but you don't
have to get old.

GEORGE BURNS

YOUTH IS THE GIFT OF NATURE, BUT AGE IS A WORK OF ART.

GARSON KANIN

It's a great thing
getting older.
You are who you are;
you say what
you mean.

REESE WITHERSPOON

I'M LIKE OLD WINE.
THEY DON'T BRING
ME OUT VERY
OFTEN, BUT I'M
WELL PRESERVED.

ROSE KENNEDY

I don't need you to
remind me of my age.
I have a bladder to
do that for me.

STEPHEN FRY

GETTING OLD IS A
FASCINATING THING.
THE OLDER YOU GET,
THE OLDER YOU
WANT TO GET!

KEITH RICHARDS

The older one
grows, the more one
likes indecency.

VIRGINIA WOOLF

GRAVITY AND
WRINKLES ARE FINE
WITH ME. THEY'RE
A SMALL PRICE TO
PAY FOR THE NEW
WISDOM INSIDE MY
HEAD AND MY HEART.

DREW BARRYMORE

You only live once,
but if you do it right,
once is enough.

MAE WEST

INSIDE EVERY OLD PERSON IS A YOUNG PERSON WONDERING WHAT HAPPENED.

ANONYMOUS

Nobody loves life
like him that's
growing old.

SOPHOCLES

THE LONGER I LIVE THE MORE BEAUTIFUL LIFE BECOMES.

FRANK LLOYD WRIGHT

Wisdom doesn't necessarily come with age. Sometimes age just shows up all by itself.

TOM WILSON

THE YOUNG SOW WILD OATS. THE OLD GROW SAGE.

HENRY JAMES BYRON

Do not worry about
avoiding temptation.
As you grow older
it will avoid you.

JOEY ADAMS

THE OLD BELIEVE EVERYTHING; THE MIDDLE-AGED SUSPECT EVERYTHING; THE YOUNG KNOW EVERYTHING.

OSCAR WILDE

I'm like a
good cheese.
I'm just getting
mouldy enough
to be interesting.

PAUL NEWMAN

I ADVISE YOU TO GO
ON LIVING SOLELY TO
ENRAGE THOSE WHO
ARE PAYING YOUR
ANNUITIES. IT IS
THE ONLY PLEASURE
I HAVE LEFT.

VOLTAIRE

I feel like I'm
so much more
interesting now [...]
I can bring so much
more to the table.

REGINA KING

I REFUSE TO ADMIT I'M MORE THAN FIFTY-TWO, EVEN IF THAT DOES MAKE MY SONS ILLEGITIMATE.

NANCY ASTOR

Live each day
as if your life
had just begun.

**JOHANN WOLFGANG
VON GOETHE**

MY BELIEF IS THAT
IT'S A PRIVILEGE TO
GET OLDER – NOT
EVERYBODY GETS
TO GET OLDER.

CAMERON DIAZ

Don't let ageing
get you down.
It's too hard
to get back up.

JOHN WAGNER

I'M AT AN AGE
WHEN MY BACK
GOES OUT MORE
THAN I DO.

PHYLLIS DILLER

Looking fifty
is great – if
you're sixty.

JOAN RIVERS

FOR ALL THE ADVANCES IN MEDICINE, THERE IS STILL NO CURE FOR THE COMMON BIRTHDAY.

JOHN GLENN

Wrinkles should
merely indicate
where the smiles
have been.

MARK TWAIN

YOUTH WOULD BE
AN IDEAL STATE IF
IT CAME A LITTLE
LATER IN LIFE.

H. H. ASQUITH

Time is a
dressmaker
specializing in
alterations.

FAITH BALDWIN

OLD AGE:
THE CROWN OF
LIFE, OUR PLAY'S
LAST ACT.

CICERO

Old age is no
place for sissies.

BETTE DAVIS

THE GOLDEN AGE
IS BEFORE US,
NOT BEHIND US.

WILLIAM SHAKESPEARE

OFFICIALLY
RETIRED

QUOTES AND
QUIPS TO CELEBRATE
YOUR FREEDOM

Officially Retired

Quotes and Quips to
Celebrate your Freedom

Hardback | 978-1-83799-212-6

Congratulations, you've retired! It's time to
celebrate your freedom. Make the most of all
your new free time with this delightful collection
quotes, quips and statements on the joys and
tribulations of retirement. Put your feet up,
relax and enjoy this side-splitting little book.

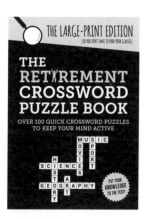

The Retirement Crossword Puzzle Book

Over 100 Quick Crossword Puzzles
to Keep Your Mind Active

Paperback | 978-1-83799-341-3

You've earned your freedom and now you have the
time, the knowledge and this book to start solving
entertaining, creative and clever crossword puzzles.
With more than 100 puzzles of varying difficulty,
plus clues and solutions, this activity book is the
perfect way to spend your new-found free time.

Have you enjoyed this book?
If so, find us on Facebook at
Summersdale Publishers,
on Twitter/X at **@Summersdale**
and on Instagram and TikTok at
@summersdalebooks
and get in touch.
We'd love to hear from you!

www.summersdale.com